RESURRECTION: MYTH OR MIRACLE?

Resurrection:
Myth or Miracle?

Robert D. Johnston

JOHN RITCHIE LTD
CHRISTIAN PUBLICATIONS

40 Beansburn, Kilmarnock, Scotland

ISBN-13: 978 1 907731 46 4

www.ritchiechristianmedia.co.uk

Typeset by John Ritchie Ltd., Kilmarnock
Printed by Bell & Bain Ltd., Glasgow

Contents

I.

THE DOCTRINE DENIED.

Now He is dead! Far hence He lies
  In the lone Syrian town;
And on His grave, with shining eyes,
  The Syrian stars look down.

So sang in dismal strains the sceptical poet, Matthew Arnold. Since his time, however, we have travelled apace, and in these present days the Resurrection of the Lord Jesus Christ is doubted and challenged, not merely by unbelieving poets, but by professedly "believing" preachers. From these it is only too common to meet with expressions of this nature: "It is no longer possible to insist on the literal accuracy of the Gospel incidents, and this is particularly true of the Virgin Birth, and of the Resurrection." Or again: "With reference to the Resurrection of Jesus . . . the appearance in Jerusalem to the two women is almost universally given up . . . The statements as to the empty sepulchre are to be rejected."

9

More recently another writer finds he must deny "the physical ascension of Christ," and calmly proceeds to tell us that "it is obvious that the bodily resurrection of Christ is intimately connected with the bodily ascension." Hence, in plain language, both must be denied. Nor is there, to such men, any truth of the Christian faith too precious to be thus pilloried, or too cherished to be thus criticised.

Before the bar of modern thought, even the great fundamental tenet of the Resurrection of Christ has been arraigned. Over it the critics have nodded their heads wisely, and then, with an air of dignified superiority, have passed sentence of condemnation upon it. Now they would have us believe that nothing more remains but duly to carry out the decree pronounced upon it, and thereafter to relegate its effigy to some theological museum, there to be wonderingly gazed upon by future generations as a relic of the cruder beliefs of a less enlightened age. And should some humbler mind have the temerity to challenge both their procedure and their decision, the critical wiseacres

can only raise their eyebrows in mild surprise,
deeming their conclusions to be above question.

*   *   *   *   *

This denial of the Resurrection is no new
thing, for the heart of man has always opposed
the truth of God. In the early history of the
Church, when Resurrection truth predominated
in her message, the strongest opposition was
offered by religious leaders. It was when
Stephen the protomartyr, put upon his defence
before the Jewish Sanhedrin, proclaimed, not
a dead Christ, but a risen and ascended Saviour,
that the hatred of his compatriots reached its
culminating point in his martyrdom. Hear him,
as before the assembled councillors silent and
sullen, he fearlessly announces : "Behold, I see
the heavens opened, and the Son of Man
standing on the right hand of God" (Acts 7.
56). This was as the spark to the tinder :
"Then they cried out with a loud voice, and
stopped their ears, and ran upon him with one
accord, and cast him out of the city, and stoned
him" (vv. 57, 58).

Some time afterward, when Paul—who had

taken up the banner of the Cross not long after
it had fallen from the hand of the dying martyr
—was preaching to the philosophic inquirers on
Mars Hill, the declaration of the same truth
provoked a similar opposition.   Said the
Apostle : "The times of this ignorance God
winked at; but now commandeth all men everywhere to repent : Because He hath appointed
a day, in the which He will judge the world
in righteousness by that man whom He hath
ordained; whereof He hath given assurance
unto all men, in that He hath raised Him
from the dead" (Acts 17. 30, 31).   Whereupon
his Athenian hearers, who, their natural curios-
ity thoroughly aroused, had hitherto listened
attentively, would hear no more.   So we read :
"When they heard of the resurrection of the
dead, some mocked" (v. 32).   And while these
scoffing Greeks have had a multitude of suc-
cessors in every age, in none have they had
more than at the present day.   For this spirit
of criticism, gathering strength numerically, has
increased in boldness.   Indeed, it has now become, in certain circles, quite fashionable not

to believe in many truths once held dear, among them what is somewhat slightingly termed "the traditional view of the Resurrection."

*   *   *   *   *

Nevertheless, it is open to serious doubt whether modern critics have ever apprehended the immense importance of the truth and teaching of the Resurrection, that they should thus lightly consign it to the scrap-heap of outworn creeds. For, like constellations round twin suns, the Resurrection and its consequent blessings all revolve round a two-fold pivot, of which the first is the power of God. When Paul, long a prisoner at Caesarea, was brought at last before Agrippa, this was his assertion : "Now I stand and am judged for the hope of the promise made of God unto our fathers" (Acts 26. 6). Then he raised the question which lies at the very core of this chief of miracles : "Why should it be thought a thing incredible with you, that God should raise the dead?" (v. 8). Or, as it might be more graphically rendered : "What! is it judged incredible with you, if God raises the dead?" Unbelief looks at *the dead*, and the difficulties are great; faith fixes its vision upon *God*, and the difficulties are gone.

But there is another pivot. It is the perfections of Christ. "We have to do with one particular Man. And when we look at the circumstances and character of this Man, while the wonderfulness of His resurrection remains, its unlikelihood vanishes." The perfections of Christ made His non-resurrection an utter impossibility; the power of God made His resurrection a glorious reality. Thrice-blessed is the soul who, rejoicing in His boundless salvation, and ravished by His matchless loveliness, can sing :

> I have seen the face of Jesus,
>   Tell me not of aught beside;
> I have heard the voice of Jesus,
>   And my soul is satisfied.
> In the radiance of the glory
>   First I saw His blessed face,
> And for ever shall that glory
>   Be my home, my dwelling-place.

II.

ITS   VAST   IMPORTANCE.

THE Resurrection of Jesus Christ is a subject of momentous import. It is either the grandest event since time was, or the greatest deception ever foisted on a credulous world. Even Strauss, an opponent of the faith, recognized its significance, and spoke of it as a "burning question." If true, it is the invincible Gibraltar of our faith; proved false, it becomes the ignoble Waterloo of our hopes. If, as some would tell us, we must relinquish the belief, then in the very act we must loosen our grasp on every other Christian truth. For Christianity is essentially and emphatically "the Gospel of the Resurrection," without which it is only a religious sentiment, an aspiration devoid of inspiration, "the expression and not the satisfaction of human need."

Read once more that transcendent fifteenth chapter of Paul's first letter to the Church at

Corinth, and judge whether Dr. Liddon be not right when he says : "Paul, writing to a Gentile Church, expressly makes Christianity answer with its life for the literal truth of the Resurrection." It is this truth which is the keystone of the arch of the Christian religion, which removed, causes the whole structure to crash, involving in its ruin five facts of priceless importance. If it must go, there goes with it

(1) THE MISSION OF CHRIST.

We are told by the modernist that "though Christ might not have been the first revelation of God, He was sent from God to comfort His fellows." The admission is that He was *a* revelation of God. But He was more. He was in a sense absolutely unique—*the* Revelation of God, "God manifest in the flesh" (1 Tim. 3. 16).

As a man's words express the thoughts of his heart, so Christ was the expression of God, and spoke out the very heart of God, throbbing with infinite compassion for a perishing world. Hence it is written of Him : "In the beginning was the Word, and the Word was with God, and the Word was God. All things were made by Him" (John 1. 1-3). But the inspired record continues: "The Word was made flesh, and dwelt among us (and we beheld His glory; the glory as of the only-begotten of the Father), full of grace and truth" (John 1. 14). None but the Son of God could adequately lay bare the heart of God, and so we read: "The only-begotten Son, which is in the bosom of the Father, He hath declared Him" (John 1. 18). His supreme purpose on earth was to reveal God to sinful men, to unfold the love of God in the sacrifice of Himself; by that one sacrifice to put away sin, and so to make it possible that men, receiving Him by faith, might have the "right to become the sons of God" (John 1. 12).

But as one has put it, "to know God as Father required that he who knows must be a son; for filial love, like parental love, is one of the basal emotions, and can only be known experimentally, not theoretically." Now, Jesus Christ declared to men, and that

B

"calmly and continuously and consistently," that He was the Son of God. But if His ashes mingled with the Syrian soil, His Sonship vanishes, the Fatherhood of God is gone, and the mission of Christ has failed miserably. Hence Paul writes : "If Christ be not risen, then is our preaching vain" (1 Cor. 15. 14).

Again, if the Resurrection goes, there goes with it

(2) THE VERACITY OF THE SCRIPTURES.

In the Old Testament it is plainly foretold, as we shall see later, that Messiah would rise from the dead. In due time, Jesus Christ appeared among men, claiming to be the Messiah, and declaring that they would put Him to death, but that He would rise again. All four of His biographers—Matthew, Mark, Luke and John—report that He did rise on the third day after His death.

In the Book of the Acts, the Resurrection is persistently affirmed. Indeed, the first recorded incident following upon the Ascension at Olivet, is the filling of the place of the arch-traitor Judas by one, Matthias, who is to be a "witness of His resurrection" (Acts 1. 22). Both the message and the manner of its proclamation are aptly described in these words: "With great power gave the Apostles witness of the Resurrection of the Lord Jesus" (Acts 4. 33).

The same theme, too, forms the basis of the Epistles, into which it is inextricably woven. Writing to believers in Rome, Paul makes it the ground of his and their assurance, saying: "Who is He that condemneth? It is Christ that died, yea rather, that is risen again, who is even at the right hand of God, who also maketh intercession for us" (Rom. 8. 34). Again, writing to the Corinthian Christians, he urges the Resurrection as the incentive to consecrated service, in these words: "For the love of Christ constraineth us; because we thus judge, that if One died for all, then were all dead: and that He died for all, that they which live should not henceforth live unto themselves, but unto Him which died for them, and rose again" (2 Cor. 5. 14, 15).

When he asserts his apostleship to the
Galatians, among whom it had been freely
challenged, he describes himself as "Paul an
apostle (not of men, neither by man, but by
Jesus Christ, and God the Father, who raised
Him from the dead)" (Gal. 1. 1). And when
to the saints at Ephesus he desires to convey
something of the abounding mercy of the God
of salvation, he reminds them that "God, who
is rich in mercy, for His great love wherewith
He loved us, even when we were dead in sins,
hath quickened us together with Christ" (Eph.
2. 4, 5).

Nor is Paul alone in this. When the Apostle
Peter writes to comfort "the strangers scattered," he confronts them with the glory of
a deathless hope, saying : "Blessed be the God
and Father of our Lord Jesus Christ, which
according to His abundant mercy hath begotten
us again unto a living hope by the resurrection
of Jesus Christ from the dead" (1 Pet. 1. 3).

Again, to John in the loneliness of his island
prison was given that glorious vision of the
Son of Man, when these reassuring words fell

upon his ear : "Fear not; I am the first and the last. I am He that liveth, and was dead; and behold I am alive for evermore, Amen" (Rev. 1. 17, 18).

Clearly, if that Resurrection must go, then the Old Testament that foretells it, the Gospels which report it, the Acts which affirms it, and the Epistles which expound it, must all go too. Therefore, as Paul writes : "If Christ be not risen, . . . we are found false witnesses" (1 Cor. 15. 14, 15).

If Christ be not risen, then is our preaching vain, and your faith is also vain. Yea, and we are found false witnesses of God: because we have testified of God that he raised up Christ; whom he raised not up, if so be that the dead rise not. For if the dead rise not, then is not Christ raised: And if Christ be not raised, your faith is vain; ye are yet in your sins. Then they also which are fallen asleep in Christ are perished. If in this life only we have hope in Christ, we are of all men most miserable. But now is Christ risen from the dead, and become the first-fruits of them that slept.

—1 Cor. 15. 14-20.

III.

MORE ABOUT ITS IMPORTANCE.

SO vastly important is the Resurrection of Jesus Christ as an intrinsic part of Christian belief, that it can neither be over-rated nor over-stated. If before the invading floods of criticism the Resurrection must be swept away, the cataclysm must involve, as we have seen, the mission of Christ, and the veracity of the Scriptures. But still the ruin is not complete. Sweep away the Resurrection, and with it goes

(3) THE ATONEMENT.

The death of a man upon a cross was no new sight. It had happened frequently before the death of our Lord Jesus Christ, and was a common occurrence after it. "An ancient historian tells us that at the siege of Babylon Darius condemned three thousand captives of war to the death of the cross. Another relates how, when Alexander inflicted long-threatened vengeance on Tyre, he crucified two thousand prisoners, and that crosses stood on her bloody shores thicker than ships' masts in a crowded harbour. And when the Romans let fly their eagles against Jerusalem, Titus, measuring out to the Jews the measure they had meted out to Jesus, gave them crosses enough."

A spectator of the scenes, amid which Judah's sun set in blood for ever, tells us that "wood was wanting for crosses and crosses for bodies." Yet of that vast multitude which in the accumulation of the years has so died, there was only One of whom it could be said : "Who His own self bare our sins in His own body on the tree" (1 Pet. 2. 24). But if Jesus Christ did not leave that virgin tomb in bodily form, His death on the Cross would have no more meaning for us, and could bring no more blessing to us, than the death of any one of those victims of Persian, Greek, or Roman cruelty. If there was no Resurrection, the work of atonement falls to pieces, and the case of humanity is hopeless beyond description. Thus, writes the Apostle: "If Christ be not raised . . . ye are yet in your sins" (1 Cor. 15. 17).

Further, if the Resurrection goes, there is likewise carried away in the crash

(4) ALL FUTURE HOPE.

Shakespeare pictures that prince of procrastinators, Hamlet, pondering over "The undiscover'd country from whose bourn no traveller returns." Of life beyond the grave, the philosophies of men hope much, but they know nothing. At best their thoughts are but "pathetic guesses." It required the "Teacher come from God" (John 3. 2), Christ Jesus the Lord, to speak to a humble company of devoted followers such words as these: "In My Father's house are many mansions: if it were not so, I would have told you. I go to prepare a place for you" (John 14. 2). But if death asserted (and has continued to maintain) its power over Him, what then is left? "A splendid guess, an inextinguishable desire, alone have sought to pierce the darkness beyond the tomb, if Jesus has not (as we believe) borne our human nature into the presence of God." For if there be no Resurrection, the light that shines upon the future life is snuffed out, and the clods, that thud with hollow reverberation on the lowered casket of that believing loved one, sound the death-knell of all our hopes. Therefore the Apostle writes : "If Christ be not raised . . . then they also which are fallen asleep in Christ are perished" (1 Cor. 15. 18).

Finally, if the Resurrection must fall to the ground, then we have a catastrophe indeed, for with it goes to pieces

(5) THE CHARACTER OF CHRIST.

In the *Glasgow Evening News,* of July 26,

1920, appeared a paragraph headed "A Resurrection Failure." It concerned Andrew Singleton, leader of the ' Holy Rollers ' sect in America, who had "exacted a death-bed promise from his wife and prominent members of his sect, that they would disinter his coffin after three months. When this was done, he had said, he would rise from the dead and greet them. A large assembly of ' Holy Rollers,' at Lexington Cemetery, watched the coffin exhumed. It was opened, but quickly closed, and re-interred." No more is added, for an obvious reason. Now, Singleton was one of two things, a knave or a fool; a knave if he were deceiving others, a fool if self-deceived. If Jesus Christ said He would rise again, to deny that He did so rise is to reduce Him to the level of Andrew Singleton. That He predicted His rising again, even His bitterest enemies were compelled to admit, for after His death, they said to Governor Pilate : "Sir, we remember that that deceiver said, while He was yet alive, 'After three days I will rise again' " (Matt. 27. 63). This He had done in unmistakable terms on seven occasions at least: (1) On beginning His ministry (John 2. 19); (2) In reply to the demand for a sign (Matt. 12. 40); (3) After Peter's confession (Matt. 16. 21); (4) Descending the Mount of Transfiguration (Mark 9. 9); (5) While abiding in Galilee (Mark 9. 31); (6) Going up to Jerusalem (Luke 18. 33); and (7) On the betrayal night (Mark 14. 28). Clearly, then, the Lord's truthfulness and honour are staked upon the Resurrection. Others before Him had claimed to be Messiah, some twelve impostors having arisen during His thirty years in Nazareth. The Resurrection was the proof, foretold by Himself that His claims were true. Accordingly, to deny the Resurrection is to bespatter His fair Name with foul calumny, a thing which His avowed enemies have ever been loth to do. Indeed, it has been far otherwise. "Cultured infidelity has vied with Christianity in admiration of His peerless excellences, in praise of His manifold virtues, in acknowledgment of His beneficent influences upon the world." But once more has He been wounded in the house of His friends, and to His avowed followers, vaunting themselves of the modern critical school, has it been reserved to do what infidels have shrunk from doing, namely, to libel Him as either a cheat or a simpleton. Such is the only possible conclusion from the denial of His resurrection. Upon either supposition the words of the Apostle are verily true: "If Christ be not raised . . . your faith is vain" (1 Cor. 15. 17).

If, therefore, it could be proved that Joseph's tomb imprisoned the body of the Lord Jesus Christ beyond the third day after His death, then the Christian faith, instead of being based upon the noblest of lives and teaching, is founded on either a great delusion, or a gross deception. On such a hypothesis, the despairing cry of the Apostle is: "We are of all men most miserable" (1 Cor. 15. 19). But both suggestions are speedily and vigorously refuted by a myriad-throated multitude of redeemed sinners in every age, who unite with

Paul in his exultant shout : *"But now is Christ
risen from the dead"* (1 Cor. 15. 20).

> Hallelujah! Christ is risen,
>   And He lives to die no more;
> To His hand the keys are given,
>   Open is the prison door.
> Hallelujah! hallelujah!
>   Now our triumph is begun;
> Death and hell are spoiled for ever,
>   And the victory is won.

IV.

FALSE THEORIES.

THERE is little in this world more ludicrous than the extravagance of thought in which men will indulge, when the rein is given to the imagination. What finely-spun speculations are given forth in all solemnity, their authors evidently omitting to notice that, if finely spun, these are correspondingly thin. In a vain attempt to explain away the fact that our Lord Jesus Christ rose from the dead on the third day, there has been invented a succession of theories of the Resurrection. Of these, five have been outstanding.

(1) THE RESUSCITATION THEORY.

This theory suggested that Jesus was not really dead, and was nursed back to life by

His disciples who thereupon declared that He had risen. To lend credence to this, the historian Josephus is quoted, in an account of a crucified officer who was thus restored. To this theory there is a threefold answer. (a) Of the reality of the death of Christ there could be no reasonable doubt. Judge Pilate was certain of it, else he would never have surrendered the body to His friends. The Jewish rulers were equally sure of it, for the intensity of their hatred would never have let go their victim while life remained. The centurion and his men were likewise positive about it, for they knew that they would be held personally responsible for the escape of their prisoner, as instance the jailer at Philippi, and yet they handed over the body. Further, to these soldiers such executions were common, and so they were accustomed to recognise when death had occurred. Besides, to make assurance doubly sure, one of them pierced His heart with a spear. (b) Again, the officer referred to, on being brought round, was a physical wreck. But the Lord Jesus Christ came forth from the tomb in the full vigour of health, scarred but unweakened. "Without an effort He stepped out of the depth of death, from under the load of sin. It was no flickering life, crucified but not killed, creeping back in a convalescence miscalled resurrection; it was the rising of the sun." Only such an appearing could have sufficed to rally the despairing and dispersing disciples, and sent them everywhere boldly proclaiming a risen Christ. (c) Moreover, had His been a case of resuscitation, instead of resurrection, Jesus knew of it, as also did His disciples. Then, in preaching that the Lord had risen, they were deliberately spreading a lie, and were guilty of the basest of frauds, Jesus Himself being the arch-impostor. On this theory, therefore, Christianity is conceived as reared upon a fraud. We are asked to believe that a religion which demands truth and righteousness, that exhorts its adherents to be "sincere and without offence" (Phil. 1. 10), to "put away lying" and to "speak every man truth with his neighbour" (Eph. 4. 25), and declares that "all liars shall

c

have their part in the lake which burneth
with fire and brimstone" (Rev. 21. 8), is itself
founded upon the greatest of lies! It would
take the credulity of a Bible critic to accept
such a proposition! Accordingly, some other
supposed explanation had to be found, and
so was devised—

(2) THE SWOON THEORY.

The exponents of this theory presumed that
Jesus, instead of dying, merely swooned, and
being laid in the cool tomb fragrant with
spices, He revived in a manner perfectly
natural, and emerged from the rock-tomb.
As an explanation of the mighty event of the
Resurrection, this theory is as hopelessly inadequate as its predecessor, and this is shown
in a fourfold way. (a) To begin with, it is
a serious impeachment of the judgment of
Pilate, and of the officer and soldiers who
were responsible for carrying out the execution,
and stamps them as woefully incompetent;
for the latter concluded that He was dead,
and the former accepted their conclusion. (b)

Besides, while it relieves the disciples of the charge of fraud, it brands them as a company of imbeciles. It preserves their integrity, but destroys their intelligence. (c) Further, it still charges the Lord Jesus with cruel deception, in that He allowed His followers to preach His resurrection, when He knew that they would have been more honestly employed in advertising the effectiveness of certain spices as a species of "smelling salts" for cases of fainting. (d) Moreover, recovery from a swoon does not account for the physical well-being of the risen Christ, for in such a case He would still have been a physical wreck. Even infidel Strauss recognized the fallacy of the theory: "It is impossible," he says, "that a being who had stolen half-dead out of the sepulchre, who crept about weak and ill, wanting medical treatment, who required bandaging, strengthening, and indulgence, could have given to the disciples the impression that He was a Conqueror over death and the grave, the Prince of life—an impression that lay at the bottom of their future ministry." Another "explana-

tion" had, therefore, to be found, and so David
Strauss himself propounded—

(3) THE MYTH THEORY.

According to this, the disciples were on the
tip-toe of expectation looking for the return
of their Master. Agog with "nervous excite-
ment," they were carried away by the "power
of imagination," and thought they saw the
Lord. The whole affair was simply visionary,
and from it arose the "myth" of the Resurrection. But this theory fails at three obvious
points. (a) It is based on an assumption
utterly false, for the disciples were not at all
expecting the Resurrection. On the contrary,
when Jesus Christ had predicted it, "they
understood none of these things" (Luke 18. 34),
and when the women from the sepulchre
announced it, "their words seemed to them
as idle tales, and they believed them not"
(Luke 24. 11). There was, therefore, no
subjective condition predisposing to such a
vision. (b) Again, while it may be possible
for one person to be the subject of a vision,

it is surely remarkable that the same vision should be experienced by numerous persons at one and the same time. Yet the risen Christ "was seen of Cephas, then of the twelve; after that He was seen of above five hundred brethren at once; . . . after that He was seen of James; then of all the apostles" (1 Cor. 15. 5-7). Moreover, the case of Cephas, or Peter, is noteworthy. Peter had denied the Lord he loved. Quietly brooding over the matter, he would doubtless magnify his fault, and charge himself with His death. He had a heavy heart and conscience, which only One could ease. Was Peter the fisherman, bold, hardy and matter-of-fact, the kind of man to be deceived, in such circumstances, by a vision? Such a theory fails utterly. As one has said: "Strauss demands for us that we give up one miracle, and substitute five hundred miracles in its place. Nothing can surpass the credulity of unbelief." (c) In the third place, this "myth" theory fails as to the time of its growth. Myths do not spring up rapidly, but are a development, a gradual process during the

elementary thought of a people. Yet here
is a supposed myth, made and accepted by
many persons within the space of three days!
Like the others, this theory is abjectly worth-
less, a miserable caricature of a marvellous
certainty. For that truth which the Word of
God proclaims, the Church of God proves,
that the Christ of the Tomb is now the Lord
of the Throne; that

> The Saviour lives, no more to die:
> He lives, our Head, enthroned on high;
> He lives triumphant o'er the grave:
> He lives eternally to save!
> He lives to still His people's fears;
> He lives to wipe away their tears;
> He lives their mansions to prepare;
> He lives to bring them safely there.

V.

FURTHER FALSE THEORIES

SEVERAL attempted "explanations" of the Resurrection have engaged our attention, each new one as lifeless and useless as its predecessor, and all alike being rejected. Another, therefore, must be found, and so we have—

(4) THE HALLUCINATION THEORY.

The author of this was a brilliant, infidel Frenchman, Ernest Renan. "The passion of an hallucinated woman," he declared, "gave to the world a resurrected God." His suggestion was that Mary, carried away by personal affection for Christ, persuaded herself that He had come and talked with her. But could Mary's "romance" have persuaded the little coterie of disciples, let alone the world, that the Resurrection was a reality? That company included Matthew, a Jewish tax-gatherer. From the very nature of his vocation, he was a most careful man, and one not readily hoaxed. Add to this his nationality, and then say whether *he* was likely to be easily deceived.

In that company, too, was Thomas, the hard-headed, matter-of-fact, unbelieving believer, who must have ocular demonstration of his beliefs. Think of the man who insists, not only on seeing the nail-prints, but on feeling them, and then say whether he would be likely to be duped by the sentimental ravings of an hysterical woman. And that company was soon to gain to its ranks a Saul, for years its most relentless enemy. Conscientious to the point of ferocity in his opposition to the teachers and teaching of the Resurrection, is it probable that he would be tricked by romantic nonsense? Of a truth, Renan's theory is woefully inadequate as an explanation. Accordingly, the ingenuity of unbelief must be still further taxed, and so there was given to the world what has been described as—

(5) THE SPIRIT THEORY.

Advanced by Keim, this conception agreed that the disciples had seen the Lord subsequent to His death, yet not in actual, bodily form, but only as a spirit! With regard to this, consider the record of one of the appearances to His followers. Says the Word : "They were terrified and affrighted, and supposed that they had seen a spirit. And He said unto them, 'Why are ye troubled? and why do thoughts arise in your hearts? Behold, My hands and My feet, that it is I Myself : handle Me and see; for a spirit hath not flesh and bones, as ye see Me have.'" And down through the years this revelation of the Son of God, and this conclusive experience of His reality, remained indelibly written on the hearts of His disciples, so that John, thrilled to the end by the wonderful memory, could write :

"That which was from the beginning, which we have heard, which we have seen with our eyes, which we have looked upon, and our hands have handled, of the Word of Life" (1 John 1. 1). But the account goes on: "And when He had thus spoken, He showed them His hands and His feet. And while they yet believed not for joy, and wondered, He said unto them: 'Have ye here any meat?' And they gave Him a piece of a broiled fish, and of an honey-comb. And He took it, and did eat before them" (Luke 24. 37-43).

Such a description, in its artless simplicity, bears the stamp of truth. To convince the disciples that His was a real, literal body, He said: "Handle Me." To prove to them that it was the very same body that had been scarred upon the Cross, and not another, He "showed them His hands and His feet." When men seek evidence of identification, they look commonly for birth-marks. The risen Lord offered such evidence in His death-marks, the marks of Golgotha. Moreover, as complete proof of His corporeality, He partook of food before them. Far from His being a spirit, the very thought of such a thing made them "terrified and affrighted" (v. 37), whereas the assurance that it was indeed their very Lord and Master in bodily presence with them, made them that "they believed not for joy" (v. 41). Yet men, in egregious folly, would rob us of the glorious Person of the risen, exalted Christ, and leave us with only some poor, conjuring "spook."

But while it was the real body of the Lord Jesus Christ, the body that was buffeted, scourged, crucified, and laid dead in a borrowed tomb, it was no longer a body subject to the limitations of time and space. At one moment the Lord could be breaking bread at supper with two disciples in the village of Emmaus, and, vanishing from their presence, could appear later among His followers in a lock-fast room. For that body had been through the portals of death. Going down into death it had been "sown a natural body," but in the triumph of resurrection it was

"raised a spiritual body" (1 Cor. 15. 44).
But this, be it noted, is vastly different from
being a spirit.

*   *   *   *   *

These, then, and such like, are the sub-
stitutes offered by philosophizing infidels in
place of the real, triumphant rising from among
the dead of our Lord and Saviour Jesus Christ.
To perishing sinners gasping for bread they
come, and, with learned benignity, offer them
a stone.   They help to lend credence to the
reported saying of Charles II. to one such
in his day: "You are a queer fellow; you
believe everything except the Bible."   With
welcome relief the believer turns from the
nebulous, fanciful words of men to rest with
assurance upon the plain, unequivocal assertion
of the Word of God that "He rose again
the third day according to the Scriptures" (1
Cor. 15. 4).   And, persuaded that the One
who slipped alongside the two care-worn disciples on that Emmaus road was none other
than "Jesus Himself" (Luke 24. 15), the be-

liever gladly joins in the song of victory:

Blest morning, whose first dawning rays
   Beheld the Son of God
Arise triumphant from the grave,
   And leave His dark abode.

Wrapped in the silence of the tomb
   The great Redeemer lay,
Till the revolving skies had brought
   The third, the appointed day.

Hell and the grave combined their force
   To hold our Lord in **vain**;
Sudden the Conqueror arose,
   And burst their feeble chain.

Complete atonement Thou hast made,
And to the utmost farthing paid
Whate'er Thy people owed.
How then can wrath on me take place,
When standing in Thy righteousness
And sheltered by Thy blood?

VI.

THE DOCTRINE DEFINED.

IT is characteristic of the modern thought to maintain the old words of the Bible, while investing them with new and dubious meanings. For this reason it becomes a necessity to be clear in our definitions, and sure of the content of the words we employ. Hence it will be useful to consider at this point the nature of the Resurrection.

In Greek mythology, Hector, about to go off to the wars, bade farewell to his wife Andromache, while nearby stood the nurse holding his child, who wept at the forbidding sight of the helmeted and plumed warrior.

The father-heart of Hector was touched by those tears. Removing the helmet, and laying aside the cause of the fear, he stood revealed in his own person, and opening his arms, received the child and kissed away its tears.

The Old Testament dispensation displayed God essentially in His might, His majesty, His sovereignty, and in the awfulness of His holiness. In the person of Jesus Christ, the Eternal Son, God laid aside, as it were, the aspects that inspire fear, and came out to a needy world in the full display of the infinitude of His love.

When men by searching had failed to "find out God," the "only-begotten Son, which is in the bosom of the Father, He hath declared Him" (John 1. 18). Our Lord Jesus Christ, who in eternity was the "express image" of God's person, became in time the perfect revelation of God's character. To effect this revelation, this unveiling, He clothed Himself with a body. While that body was in every sense real, it was a body prepared by God. Hence the Scripture records: "When He cometh into the world, He saith, 'Sacrifice and offerings Thou wouldest not, but a body hast Thou prepared Me'" (Heb. 10. 5).

Since He was essentially and eternally God, that body was the only part of Him that could die. With that body He went to the Cross, and that body did die. "Wicked hands" crucified and slew Him, but it was because He had been "delivered by the determinate counsel and foreknowledge of God" (Acts 2. 23).

*　　*　　*　　*　　*

Neither men nor demons possessed power of death over Christ. As a "sacrifice for sins" He offered His body (Heb. 10. 11, 12), willingly laying down His life, as He had declared He would, saying : "Therefore doth My Father love Me, because I lay down My life, that I might take it again. No man taketh it from Me, but I lay it down of Myself. I have power to lay it down, and I have power to take it again" (John 10. 17, 18). His death was as His life, in perfect subjection to the will of God the Father, for

D

He became "obedient unto death" (Phil. 2. 8).

But while that body, dishonoured and cruci-fied by men, died and was laid in the grave, it could not see corruption (Acts 2. 27), and rose from the dead. With the body which He had taken in incarnation Christ died, and with that very body He came forth from the tomb on the third day. For the body which tender hands had wrapped around with the garments of the grave, and laid among the fragrant embalming spices in the rock sepulchre, was not to be found there when sought.

As He had died bodily, so He had risen again bodily. "The grave in which His torn body lay was sealed with the authority of Rome, and Roman soldiers kept guard over it. And yet neither the power of death, nor the armed strength of Rome, nor the hate of the Jewish Sanhedrin, could keep that grave sealed. Life came back to the torn body, the seal of Rome on the tomb was broken, and the risen Christ came out victorious over death."

Vain the stone, the watch, the seal,
Christ has burst the gates of hell;
Death in vain forbids His rise,
Christ has opened Paradise.

This, and nothing less than this, was the
Resurrection proclaimed by Paul, for writing
to Timothy he says : "Remember that Jesus
Christ *of the seed of David* was raised from
the dead according to my Gospel" (2 Tim. 2.
8), thus linking the Resurrection with the
physical descent of the Lord Jesus.   This, too,
was the Resurrection the apostles preached,
for the Sadducees, who denied a literal raising
of the body, "came upon them, being grieved
that they taught the people, and preached
through Jesus the resurrection from the dead"
(Acts 4. 1, 2).

Besides, nothing but a real, literal, bodily
resurrection meets the deep needs of weak
and sinning humanity.   Just as at a later time
the earthquake opening the prison doors was
the "Amen" of God to the prayers and praises
of Paul and Silas, so the raising of Jesus
Christ from the prison-house of death was

God's "Amen" to that shout of triumph on
the Cross, "It is finished." It was God's seal
set for ever to the atoning work of the Cross.
It was His avowal to the universe that the
work demanded by His unsullied holiness and
unswerving righteousness had been perfectly
completed. It was His receipt for the price
of our redemption, freely and fully paid, en-
abling the believing sinner to say with a
heaven-begotten confidence :

> Complete atonement Thou hast made,
> And to the utmost farthing paid
> Whate'er Thy people owed.
> How then can wrath on me take place,
> When standing in Thy righteousness
> And sheltered by Thy blood?

*   *   *   *   *

Hence it was that Peter, in Jerusalem's
streets on that wonderful Pentecost morning,
preached a crucified Christ, adding, "Whom
God hath raised up, having loosed the pains
of death, because it was not possible that He
should be holden of it" (Acts 2. 24). This
word "pains" is a very significant word. It is

a word translated elsewhere "sorrows" (Matt. 24. 8), and "travail" (1 Thess. 5. 3), and means "birth-pangs." As one puts it: "The very pangs of death, that held the Son of God, became the birth-pangs of a new creation."

The word "loosed" is likewise pregnant with meaning and suggestiveness. It is rendered in the New Testament variously, the different expressions together serving to illustrate the perfection of power that God exerted in the raising-up of His Son. It is used of the loosing of a tied colt (Mark 11. 2); of the taking down of the stones of a building (John 2. 19); of the putting off of shoes (Acts 7. 33); and of the breaking up of a ship (Acts 27. 41). It is employed, too, for the breaking of the marriage tie by death (1 Cor. 7. 27); for the removing of a hindrance (Eph. 2. 14); for the destroying of the works of the enemy (1 John 3. 8); and for the releasing of a prisoner (Rev. 20. 7).

And this full expression of the thoroughness of the Resurrection of Jesus Christ is at the same time God's perfect vindication of His sacrificial work; so that the believer, gazing first at the Cross, and then at the empty tomb, can sing:

> Thus, while His death my guilt displays
>   In all its blackest hue,
> Such is the mystery of grace,
>   It seals my pardon, too.

VII.

THE TRUTH ASSERTED.

IN the introductory verses of the Book of Acts, we are told that to the Apostles Jesus showed Himself alive after His Passion by many infallible proofs (1. 3). The word here employed is interesting. It is that used in Aristotle's "Logic," for "demonstrative proofs." It is related to the word for "an end, a goal, a fixed boundary," and signifies that nothing more in the way of proof can be given. Since the Word of God asserts, and reiterates again and again, the fact of the Resurrection of Christ, and since "all Scripture is given by inspiration of God" (2

Tim. 3. 16), the last word has been spoken.

It is surely a sign of the times, however, that men who readily accept the historicity of the old-world celebrities upon the evidence of a few writers, cavil at the traditional teachings about our Lord Jesus Christ, although these are attested by a much greater mass of evidence. Indeed, very few facts, if any, of such a remote date, are supported by such a great amount of evidence as is the Resurrection. We might even go further, and agree with Westcott that, "taking all the evidence together, it is not too much to say that there is no single historic incident better or more variously supported than the Resurrection of Christ. Nothing but the antecedent assumption that it must be false could have suggested the idea of deficiency in the proof of it."

ELEVEN APPEARANCES.

During the forty days before His Ascension, eleven appearances of Christ are recorded, involving not fewer than five hundred witnesses.

He appeared to Mary (John 20. 14); to the other women (Matt. 28. 1-9); to Peter (1 Cor. 15. 5); to two disciples on the Emmaus road (Luke 24. 13-32); to the disciples in the absence of Thomas; to them with Thomas present (John 20. 24-29); to certain disciples at the Sea of Tiberias (John 21. 1-14); to the eleven in Galilee (Matt. 28. 16-20); to over five hundred brethren (1 Cor. 15. 6); to James (1 Cor. 15. 7); and finally, to all the Apostles at His Ascension (Acts 1. 9, 10). Accordingly, Peter could say: "Him God raised up the third day, and showed Him openly; not to all the people, but unto witnesses chosen before of God, even to us, who did eat and drink with Him after He rose from the dead" (Acts 10. 40).

Moreover, not only are the witnesses very numerous, but they are in the highest degree reliable. Said Sir Isaac Newton: "I find more sure marks of authenticity in the New Testament, than in any profane history whatever." The historian Rawlinson adds his testimony thus: "In truth, there is not the slightest pretence for insinuating that there ever was any doubt as to the authorship of any one of the historical books of the New Testament . . . There is, indeed, far better evidence of authorship in the case of the four Gospels and of the Acts of the Apostles, than exists with respect to the works of almost any classical writer."

WITNESS OF OPPONENTS.

The very enemies of the Christian faith have borne witness to this. It was John Stuart Mill, atheistic philosopher, who wrote : "It is of no use to say that Christ as exhibited in the Gospels, is not historical. . . Who among His disciples or among their proselytes was capable of inventing the sayings ascribed to Jesus, or of imagining the life and character revealed in the Gospels?" Another infidel, the Frenchman Jean Jaques Rousseau, is the author of these words : "Shall we suppose the evangelical history a mere fiction? Indeed, my friend, it bears no mark of fiction. On the contrary, the history of Socrates, which no one presumes to doubt, is not so well attested as that of Jesus Christ."

Nevertheless, let us begin with the admitted fact that we possess four records of the Resurrection of Christ. Who wrote them, or when they were written, is not material to our argument. History written as it is being made is frequently somewhat biased, and to that extent false, whereas history set down after the event sees it in more correct perspective. The four records are plainly either true or false. If they are false, then they were invented. If they were invented, they were so either by the writers in collusion, or by them independently. Now, these four accounts do not exactly and entirely agree, but show differences. These divergencies, moreover, are too numerous and too apparent for the accounts to have been composed together.

On the other hand, these four records agree in the salient facts of the event. "They all affirm that Jesus actually died upon the Cross, not in a swoon betokening physical and mental exhaustion and weakness, but crying with a loud voice, and hence in possession of all His faculties. They all affirm that His body was given by Pilate to Joseph, although John adds that Nicodemus joined him in the last rites of respect to the dead. They all affirm that the body was laid in a new sepulchre, three of them mentioning the great stone that was placed at its entrance. They all affirm that He rose from the dead on the first day of the week, and that the sepulchre was found to be empty."

Since these agreements of detail are so many and so distinctive, it is very evident that the narratives could not have been invented independently. If, therefore, their variations exclude the possibility of these four accounts having been concocted together, and if their harmonies debar the idea of their having been made up separately, the only possible conclusion is, that they were not made up at all, but were the records of facts as they actually occurred.

INCONSISTENCY OF CRITICS.

But no critics are so inconsistent as Bible critics. If these accounts of the Resurrection of our Lord had agreed, word for word and point for point, then swifter than the vulture to its prey would the critics have swooped down to accuse the writers of "fraudulent conspiracy with intent to deceive." When they do not agree in this fashion, these same critics triumphantly proclaim them to be contradictory and incorrect, and consequently not inspired. How plain it is to minds delivered, in the mercy of God, from that criticism which is a compound of sinful pride, presumption, and prejudice, that had the Gospel stories of the Resurrection been invented by men, they would have been made appear to agree, and discrepancies would have been detected only by careful scrutiny. Whereas, in these accounts, the seeming discrepancies lie patent to the gaze of all, while the real agreement, the harmony. of purpose, lies latent underneath the surface. Happy is he who, heedless of the vain philosophies and vapid theorisings of men, and believing implicitly the "record of God concerning His Son," finds peace only in "the blood of His Cross," and stands before God only in the righteousness imputed to us "if we believe on Him that raised up Jesus our Lord from the dead" ((Rom. 4. 24).

VIII.

INTERNAL EVIDENCE.

IT is intensely interesting to examine in detail
the Scripture accounts of the circumstances
attending the resurrection of the Lord Jesus
Christ, and to observe in them the marks of
their inherent truthfulness which everywhere
abound. We proceed to consider some of
them.

(1) Had these narratives been invented, the
authors would assuredly have related how
Christ appeared to His followers; and, to put
them above the charge of having been mistaken,
they would have pictured Him with them con-

stantly, that the charge of false identity might become impossible. Yet the Gospels tell only of occasional appearances, the very thing a writer of fiction would have avoided. And why is this so? The answer is that they were not inventing a story that would *seem* true, but were recording events that *were* true.

(2) Again, had some writer been describing such happenings, knowing they were unreal, but desiring to give them an air of reality, he would certainly have avoided making Christ appear only to friends, knowing that this would weaken his evidence, friends not being impartial witnesses. How graphic it would have been to make Him step from the tomb in the garden, gather His disciples, and ride triumphantly through Jerusalem, with a wondering throng in His wake! Then he would have depicted a sensational appearance to Caiaphas, the High Priest who had condemned Him. He would have made Him walk into the palace of Herod, who had mocked Him. He would have pictured Him dramatically confronting weak, vacillating Pilate, the Roman Governor,

who had sanctioned His crucifixion. Yet the
Gospel accounts tell of none of these things.
Instead, they do the very thing a writer of
fiction would not have done, and tell of His
being seen only by His friends, with not a
single appearance to enemies. And why is
this? The answer is that the writers were not
inventing scenes for effect, but were recording
events exactly as they transpired.

Unrecognised by Disciples.

(3) Further, had a writer been making up
the story that it might be accepted as a fact,
it is certain he would have made his witnesses
quite positive in their recognition of the risen
Christ. Failure in identification is at once fatal
to a case. Yet the Gospel writers state plainly
that He was not recognized at first by His
disciples. When He overtook two of them
wearily wending their way toward Emmaus,
"their eyes were holden that they should not
know Him" (Luke 24. 16). When the tear-
bedimmed Mary sought His body, she "saw

E

Jesus standing, and knew not that it was Jesus"
(John 20. 14). And when the Lord stood on
Galilee's shore, "the disciples knew not that
it was Jesus" (John 21. 4). Why do the
writers state these very points that would ruin
evidence of identification, and would be care-
fully avoided by a writer of fiction? Again,
there is only one reply possible. They were
not writing fiction, but recording facts.

(4) Peter and John, having learned of the
missing body, made for the tomb. "So they
ran both together : and the other disciple did
outrun Peter, and came first to the sepulchre;
and he, stooping down and looking in, saw
the linen clothes lying, yet went he not in.
Then cometh Simon Peter following him, and
went into the sepulchre" (John 20. 4-6). Now,
consider the character of each of these men.
John is a man of affectionate disposition, "that
disciple whom Jesus loved." So retiring is
he that he withholds his name in his writings.
He is a person of finer feelings, in whom
reverence and awe are strongly developed.
Impelled by love, he reached the sepulchre

first. Restrained by reverence, he peered in,
but paused without. Peter, on the other hand,
was bluff and hearty, bold and impetuous,
even to the point of rashness. He it was
who, when the Lord foretold His suffering
and death, burst out with the words: "Be
it far from Thee, Lord"; who, when the
soldiers had surrounded his Master, drew his
sword to defend Him. Impulsive ever, he
reaches the tomb, and at once hastens in.
Is this made up, or is it true to the characters
of these two men as we know them?

The Linen Clothes.

(5) In the same chapter, verses 6 and 7, we
are informed that Peter saw "the linen clothes
lie, and the napkin that was about His head,
not lying with the linen clothes, but wrapped
together in a place by itself." What writer
of fiction would have dreamed of taking special
notice of the napkin in such a way? Writers
only introduce points with a purpose, which
purpose is evident in the narrative, and this

description is not what they would have written. Why is it mentioned, then? The answer again is that it is what was actually seen. Yet there was something about these grave-clothes of eternal moment, that produced the statement that whereas Peter saw "the linen clothes lie," John "saw and believed" (John 20. 5-8). What was there to inspire belief? Says Dean Alford: "The word rendered 'grave-clothes' is explained to mean a sort of band or tow, used to swathe infants." Again, the word translated "lying" and "lie" (v. 5 and 6), is the word used in John 2. 6: "There were *set* there six waterpots of stone"; and in John 19. 29: "Now there was *set* a vessel filled with vinegar." It occurs, too, in Revelation 21. 16, where we are told that "the city *lieth* foursquare." The word suggests orderliness, calm deliberateness of action. Just as on a former occasion, the sleeping Christ rose, and rebuked the storm into a great calm, so from the grave-clothes that surrounded His body lying in the sleep of death, He rose in the quiet dignity of triumphant majesty, leaving His very shape in the cerements of the tomb.

(6) Once more, in John 21. 15, 16, we hear the risen Lord address Peter: "Simon, son of Jonas, lovest thou Me more than these?" Says Peter: "Yea, Lord, Thou knowest that I love Thee." Again Christ speaks: "Simon, son of Jonas, lovest thou Me?" And again comes the answer from Peter: "Yea, Lord, Thou knowest that I love Thee." Then we read: "He saith unto him the third time, 'Lovest thou Me?' And he said unto Him, 'Lord, Thou knowest all things; thou knowest that I love Thee.'" Again we ask, is this merely the product of some fertile mind? If so, what is the purpose of this thrice-repeated question? The answer is that this description is a true record of the actual facts. To know the force of it, read the tragic actions of Peter in Luke, chapter 22, which culminate in verse 61: "And the Lord turned and looked upon Peter: and Peter remembered the words of the Lord, how He

had said unto him, 'Before the cock-crow, thou shalt deny me *thrice.*' "

"HE IS RISEN."

(7) Take one final incident. The women had been to the sepulchre, and found the body of the Lord gone. The wonderful words had resounded in their ears : "He is risen; He is not here; behold the place where they laid Him" (Mark 16. 6). Then was entrusted to them this message : "Go your way, tell His disciples and Peter that He goeth before you into Galilee" (Mark 16. 7). Once more, is this imaginary or real? If it is an invention, why does the writer say, "His disciples *and Peter*"? There must be redundancy here. Surely Peter is already a disciple, and a chief one, too? But this is no fiction. It is the reality of life. It is a gracious Lord's reassurance to a trembling, wondering disciple, who denied Him, and deserted Him in His neediest hour. "Though you did deny Me, Peter," the message would say, "still you

are numbered with My disciples, and when I meet them in Galilee, I wish to meet *you* there also." Therefore the messenger says, "Go, tell His disciples and Peter."

Let the honest reader ponder those passages, and then say whether they look like fiction, or whether they bear the very impress of truth. And these are part of the records which announce the resurrection of our Lord and Saviour Jesus Christ.

The Rising from the dead of Jesus Christ was the prime truth of the Apostles' preaching.

IX.

EXTERNAL EVIDENCE OF THE RESURRECTION.

WE proceed to consider the external or circumstantial evidence of the reality of the resurrection of our Lord. In this type of evidence, we have some indisputable result, of which the fact we desire to prove is the only conceivable cause; or some admitted facts which find their only explanation in the fact whose truthfulness we seek to establish. Such evidence, far from being weak, is often the most convincing it is possible to have.

For example, some time ago a burglary was committed in a Scottish town. Outside the window of the burgled premises, two buttons were found. A house was visited of a man observed in the vicinity earlier in the evening. There the police found a garment from which two buttons were missing, and on which the remaining buttons were similar to those picked up. In the house, too, a torn piece of an account was discovered, and in the burgled premises a corresponding piece was found, the two pieces fitting exactly. No witnesses saw the burglary, yet this man was convicted and punished for the crime, entirely upon circumstantial evidence. With regard to the Resurrection there are three great proofs of this character.

The Chief Theme.

(1.) *The rising from the dead of Jesus Christ was the prime truth of the Apostles' preaching.* From the beginning it was their chief theme, their message everywhere being not only "Jesus," but also "the Resurrection." It became "the cause, the centre, and the circumference of the testimony of the early Church." It was when the Jews heard Peter preach a crucified Christ, now risen, that "they were pricked in their heart, and said unto Peter and to the rest of the Apostles, 'Men and brethren, what shall we do?'" (Acts 2. 37). Then this wonderful result followed: "The same day there were added unto them about three thousand souls" (v. 41). Contrast this with our own time, when denial of the Resurrection is coincident with the absence of concern on the part of the world, and decreasing instead of increasing numbers on the part of the professed Church. It was this same Peter who, accompanied by John, after the healing of the lame beggar, preached to the people in Solomon's Porch not a dead Christ, but One "whom God hath raised from the dead" (Acts 3. 15); adding this magnificent tribute: "And His name through faith in His name hath made this man strong; whom ye see and know: yea, the faith which is by Him hath given him this perfect soundness in the presence of you all" (v. 16). Perfect soundness can only come through a perfect Saviour; and the impotence of a race morally lamed by sin can be cured, never by the Jesus of Modernism, but ever by the omnipotence of the risen Son of God.

Moreover, these disciples, who preached the Resurrection, had the most intimate knowledge of their subject. If it were true, they knew it to be so; if false, they likewise knew it. They were men of probity, against whose character no accusation has ever been brought. The gravest charge which was made against them was that they stuck to their text. They preached a risen Christ, and refused to desist from their theme. Further, they persistently urged on others the necessity for righteousness. Is it thinkable that they themselves were busy promulgating a lie? To imagine this, is to suppose that men, guilty of the foulest of frauds, and the basest of lies, set out, by means of these, to make the world honest and truthful, and that indeed wherever their message has been accepted, this desired and desirable result has been attained!

What Did the Apostles Gain?

Besides, what was the promised gain from such an attempt? They gained poverty, loss of friends, exile from home, disgrace, dishonour, sufferings, hatred, and death. One of them could write: "Even unto this present hour, we both hunger and thirst, and are naked, and are buffeted, and have no certain dwelling-place; and labour, working with our own hands; being reviled, we bless; being persecuted, we suffer it; being defamed, we entreat; we are made as the filth of the world, and are the off-scouring of all things unto this day" (1 Cor. 4: 11-13). If the Resurrection was a fiction, then to preach this fiction what a price Paul had to pay! "In labours more abundant, in stripes above measure, in prisons more frequent, in deaths oft. Thrice was I beaten with rods, once was I stoned, thrice I suffered shipwreck, a night and a day I have been in the deep; in journeyings often, in perils of waters, in perils of robbers, in perils by mine own countrymen, in perils by the heathen, in perils in the city, in perils in the wilderness, in perils in the sea, in perils among false brethren; in weariness and painfulness, in watchings often, in hunger and thirst, in fastings often, in

cold and nakedness" (2 Cor. 11. 23-27). Would
Paul and the other disciples endure all this
to preach a fictitious resurrection, to bolster
up a fraud? The whole idea is morally
impossible, and the very suggestion an absurdity.

Moreover, in preaching the Resurrection of
Jesus Christ, the disciples pledged their honour
on a doctrine which, had it been untrue, could
easily have been disproved. There was no
denying that Jesus had been crucified, for
"this thing was not done in a corner." If
He had not risen, His dead body was some-
where. Now, it was either in the possession
of His friends, or of His foes. If it was
in the hands of His friends, who, nevertheless,
preached that He had risen, the whole thing
was a cruel deception, which, we have concluded, is a moral impossibility. The alternative
is that His body was in the hands of His
enemies. Why, then, did they not produce
the body, and confound the new faith? When,
on the day of Pentecost, Peter and his col-
leagues stood in the crowded streets of that

very city where the Crucifixion had taken place, and preached Jesus Christ, whom the Jews had "taken and by wicked hands crucified and slain; whom God hath raised up" (Acts 2. 23, 24), with such effect that three thousand converts were made, what an opportunity for these enemies! They had but to produce the body, unmask the imposture, discredit the Apostles, and preserve those three thousand persons for Judaism!

Further, there was no man in all Judea more hated than Saul of Tarsus after his conversion. Yet, writing to the Church at Corinth, this man affirmed the truth of the Resurrection, and cited over five hundred witnesses, "of whom," he wrote, "the greater part remain unto this present" (1 Cor. 15. 6). Surely here was the psychological moment, when, with one blow, they could have crushed both the hated renegade, and the obnoxious faith. Nor would this have been a difficult task. The most advanced critics put the date of this Epistle at 55 A.D., that is, only some twenty years after the "alleged" Resurrection.

If it were all a fabrication, why were not these two hundred and fifty odd witnesses summoned, and the story contradicted? But they were not, for the simple reason that the "alleged" Resurrection could not be confuted, the facts being precisely as asserted by the Apostles. There was, indeed, one piece of opposing evidence, but it was offered by some men who testified to events which, they declared, occurred while they were fast asleep! (Matt. 28. 11-14). It is to be hoped that even the critics would be inclined to reject such evidence, even though that rejection should leave, as it does leave, the stupendous fact of the Resurrection rearing itself as an eternal and invincible stronghold, far above the mists and wreckage of time.

X.

FURTHER EXTERNAL EVIDENCE OF THE RESURRECTION.

HAVING considered the evidence presented by the fact that the Resurrection was the outstanding theme in the message of the early Church, we turn now to *the second great proof, namely, the change, at the time when the Resurrection was alleged, of the accepted day of rest.* From a few months after the emancipation of the nation from Egypt's thraldom, the sacred day of the week to the Jews was Saturday. The first day of the week was not recognized by them, nor is it even now. Yet that time-honoured day of observance was changed by the disciples of Christ—who, be it remembered, were of Jewish nationality—to the first day of the week, with no special divine mandate to effect the change.

F

Now, to alter any national institution sanctioned by the centuries is most difficult of accomplishment. During the French Revolution, attempts were made to destroy the Sunday, and transform the calendar, but both were signal failures. Yet here was such an institution, a weekly day of observance that for many hundreds of years had been part of the very warp and woof of the nation, changed, as if by general consent, from the seventh to the first day of the week, to be observed ever since as the Lord's Day. Only an event of the greatest moment could have so quickly and so thoroughly effected this transition, and that event was the Resurrection.

THE LORD'S SUPPER.

Moreover, it was His dying wish that His death should be kept green in the memory of His disciples, by their partaking of bread representing His broken body, and wine speaking of His shed blood. Now, men commemorate an event upon the anniversary of the day on which it occurred, hence we should observe the Lord's Supper upon a Friday, the day of His crucifixion. Yet for fully nineteen centuries the Christian Church has commemorated that crucifixion and death on a day when it did not happen, namely, on Sunday. How, then, came that to be so? The answer is that on Sunday, the first day of the week, God's crowning glory to the death of His Son took place, in His raising Him from the dead.

In the Book of Acts—a book admitted by Renan to be authentic, and whose date he fixed at 80 A.D., some forty years after the Resurrection—we read of the disciples coming together on the first day of the week to break bread (Acts 20. 7). Again, in 1 Corinthians, admitted by Strauss to have been written within twenty-five years after the death of Jesus Christ, Paul instructs that the church collection be taken on the first day of the week (1 Cor. 16. 1, 2), which day John in the Revelation describes as "the Lord's Day" (1. 10). As Dr. Brooks points out, this change is verified by the early historians.

Barsedanes, in a letter to the philosophic emperor, Marcus Aurelius, wrote : "Lo! where-ever we be, all of us are called by the one name of the Messiah—Christians; and upon one day, which is the first day of the week, we assemble ourselves together." Later, Justin Martyn stated : "On the day called Sunday is an assembly of all who live either in the cities or in the rural districts, and the memoirs of the apostles and the writings of the prophets are read . . . because Jesus Christ our Saviour rose from the dead upon it." If, therefore, as some would have us believe, the Lord did not rise from the dead on the first day of the week, then the Christian Church has, week by week since its inception, been observing a day upon which nothing in particular transpired. In such a case, this acknowledged change of day remains unex-plained, and we are faced with an effect without a cause. But the Christian Church has not been thus deceived, and the effect has an adequate cause, for on that day the God of peace "brought again from the dead our Lord Jesus, that Great Shepherd of the sheep" (Heb. 13. 20). And only in the light of this Resurrection do the two great Christian sacraments, baptism and the Lord's Supper, find their meaning. Says Paul concerning the first : "We are buried with Him by baptism unto death : that like as Christ was raised up from the dead by the glory of the Father, even so we also should walk in newness of life" (Rom. 6. 4). Of the second he quotes the very words of the Lord, revealed expressly to himself : "As often as ye eat this bread, and drink this cup, ye do show the Lord's death *till He come*" (1 Cor. 11. 26). Except the Resurrection, and these two sacred cere- monies become as meaningless as the veriest mumbo-jumboism of darkest heathendom; ac- cept it, they thrill with divine love and life.

Transformation of the Disciples.

But perhaps the most striking of the evid- ences of the Resurrection is *the moral trans- formation in the disciples themselves*. At the arrest in the garden, they all "forsook Him and fled" (Matt. 26. 56). In the hall of Caiaphas, their very leader three times denied that he knew Him, emphasizing his declaration, by oaths and curses (Matt. 26. 69-75). At the crucifixion, they were in blank despair. The two, bending their sorrowful steps from the seat of His and their activities towards the village of Emmaus, lamented: "We trusted that it had been He which should have redeemed Israel" (Luke 24. 21). Truly, the Shepherd had been smitten and the sheep scattered indeed! But observe those same men very shortly afterwards. Dismay had given place to exultation, and they went forth to conquer the world.

Take the wonderful case of Peter. One early morn he stood, a craven coward, shivering before the accusing finger of a serving-girl in the high priest's hall. Less than two months later, this same man faced a multitude thronging Jerusalem's streets, and boldly declared about "Jesus of Nazareth"; "Him . . . ye have taken and by wicked hands have crucified and slain: Whom God hath raised up"

(Acts 2. 23, 24). In the precincts of the Temple, after the healing of a lame man, he addressed the quickly-assembling crowd, saying: "Ye denied the Holy One and the Just, and desired a murderer to be granted unto you; and killed the Prince of Life, whom God hath raised from the dead; whereof we are witnesses" (Acts 3. 14, 15). When, for the sole offence of preaching the Resurrection, Peter and John were brought next day before the very council that had condemned Jesus to death, Peter again preached to them "Jesus Christ of Nazareth, whom ye crucified, whom God raised from the dead" (Acts 4. 10). Indeed, so amazing was their boldness, that these very councillors marvelled (Acts 4. 13). They decided, however, to forbid these disciples to preach further in that Name, to which Peter and John replied thus: "Whether it be right in the sight of God to hearken unto you more than unto God, judge ye. For we cannot but speak the things which we have seen and heard" (Acts 4. 19, 20). Nor did the threats of the council deter them from their purpose, for they left that council-chamber, and the record of their subsequent activities is this: "They spake the word of God with boldness" (Acts 4. 31; cf. Acts 4. 33).

A MORAL MIRACLE.

When, later, these same apostles, with the others, were arrested and imprisoned, they refused, even with the shadow of death looming over them, to cease preaching this doctrine, for said they: "We ought to obey God rather than men. The God of our fathers raised up Jesus, whom ye slew and hanged on a tree. Him hath God exalted with His right hand to be a Prince and a Saviour" (Acts 5. 29-31). What could inspire these men, so as to transform abject cowardice into utter fearlessness? Could conscious deception, could a deliberate falsehood thus change men? Such a thought is absurdity itself. There could be but one cause, a cause all-inclusive and all-sufficient, and that was the rising again from the dead of their Saviour and Lord. Even the critic F. C. Baur is forced to this admission: "Nothing but the miracle of the Resurrection could disperse the doubts which threatened to banish the faith of the disciples into the eternal night." And here are the words of the late Lord Salisbury: "To me the central point is the Resurrection of Christ, which I believe, firstly, because it is testified by men who had every opportunity of seeing and knowing, and whose veracity was tested by the most tremendous trials, both of energy and endurance, during long lives; secondly, because of the marvellous effect it had upon the world. As a moral phenomenon, this spread and mastery of Christianity is without a parallel."

The basis for the faith of the believer.

Vindicated the Deity of Jesus Christ.

The Resurrection is the evidence of a future, yet certain, judgment upon all who reject Jesus Christ.

Moreover, the Resurrection is the token that those very persons, who, as sinners, are destined to stand at that judgment bar, can, through believing in Jesus, be justified from all things, and stand righteous before God.

XI

FRUITS OF THE RESURRECTION.

A<small>S</small> yon eastern morning sun, rising in renewed splendour, bedecks the earth with beauty and invests it with might, so in the glory of the Resurrection the Sun of Righteousness rose with healing in His wings, radiating to the sons of men moral loveliness and spiritual power. For out of the valley of the shadow of death the triumphant Son of God has borne fruits infinitely richer than the grapes from Eshcol's vale, and these we will now consider in a precious sevenfold cluster.

(1) The rising again of the Lord Jesus Christ was conclusive proof, if proof was needed, of the existence of God, and so *provided a secure basis for the faith of the believer.* Hence Peter could say that we "by Him do believe in God, that raised Him up from the dead and gave Him glory" (1 Peter

1. 21). For ages, philosophers had vainly tried "by searching" to "find out God." but when Jesus Christ came into the world, God stood revealed, for "the only-begotten Son, which is in the bosom of the Father, He hath declared Him" (John 1. 18). And the God He set forth was the God of the Bible. From the beginning of time, a continuous stream of humanity had been swallowed up by death. Jesus Christ appeared on this earth, declaring that He, too, would die, and that at the hands of men, but that God would raise Him again.

God's Personality and Power.

By the Resurrection of Christ, God displayed both His personality and His power; and the Christian can rejoice that belief in the God of the Bible is not "a figment of fancy, but is a fixed faith resting upon a firm fact." Contemplating a risen Christ, we learn "what is the exceeding greatness of His power to us-ward who believe, according to the working of His mighty power, which He wrought in

Christ, when He raised Him from the dead, and set Him at His own right hand in the heavenly places" (Eph. 1. 19, 20).

(2) *The Resurrection for ever vindicated the Deity of Jesus Christ.* During His sojourn upon earth, He asserted that He was the Son of God, but men doubted and disbelieved Him. "If Thou be the Christ, tell us plainly," they said (John 10. 24). "If Thou be Christ, save Thyself and us," repeated the dying robber (Luke 23. 39). But the Apostle states that He "was declared to be (or, marked off as) the Son of God with power, according to the spirit of holiness, by the resurrection from the dead" (Rom. 1. 4).

There are some who would rob Him of His deity, while acclaiming Him as a great Teacher. But listen to His teaching: "My doctrine is not Mine, but His that sent Me" (John 7. 16). On another occasion He said: "I have not spoken of Myself; but the Father which sent Me, He gave Me a commandment, what I should say, and what I should speak" (John 12. 49). He maintained, therefore, that His words including His announcements of His death and resurrection, were the very words of God. Then was such a stupendous claim justified? For answer, gaze into that tomb, mark the place where His body had lain, and strain your ear to catch the triumphant angel-message: "He is not here; for He is risen, as He said" (Matt. 28. 6).

Further, many in the folly of unbelief would allow Jesus Christ to be *a* Son of God, but only in the sense, they would tell us, in which all men are sons of God. But what He claimed was something entirely unique. While He spoke of the prophets as servants, Himself He called a Son (Mark 12. 6). Again, He declared: "I and My Father are one" (John 10. 30), and taught that "all men should honour the Son, even as they honour the Father" (John 5. 23).

THE ONLY-BEGOTTEN SON.

Who of the sons of men dare utter words like these: "He that hath seen Me hath seen the Father"? (John 14. 9). Five times, all in John's writings, He is called the "Only-begotten" (John 1. 14, 18; 3. 16, 18; 1 John 4. 9). The significance of this expression becomes clear when we consider its other usages. For example, in Hebrews 11. 17, Isaac is termed an "only-begotten" son. In the strict sense of the words, he was not an only son, for there was Ishmael. But he was a specially-favoured, a well-beloved son. The same word is found in Luke 7. 12, in the story of the raising of a dead youth, "the only son of his mother"; in Luke 8. 42, where Jairus is said to have had "one only daughter"; and in Luke 9. 38, where a man besought Jesus for his child, saying: "He is mine only child." Only the Lord Jesus Christ is ever called "the Only-begotten Son" of God; that is, He was in a unique sense the "only" and "well-beloved" Son.

There is another word used of Him, occurring also five times over. He is described as being the "First-begotten of creation" (Col. 1. 15; Heb. 1. 6); as the "First-begotten from the dead" (Col. 1. 18; Rev. 1. 5); and as the

"First-begotten among many brethren" (Rom.
8. 29). In association with the first creation,
the material universe, and with the new
creation, the redeemed Church, He is the
"First-begotten"; but alone in solitary relation
to God the Father, He is the Only-begotten"
Son. *In* His resurrection, He became the "first-
begotten from the dead"; *by* His Resurrection,
He was proved to be what He ever had been,
the "Only-begotten" Son of God.

(3) *The Resurrection is the evidence of a
future, yet certain, judgment upon all who reject Jesus Christ.* As He walked among men,
He declared: "The Father judgeth no man,
but hath committed all judgment unto the Son"
(John 5. 22). Further, He claimed that the
Father had "given Him authority to execute
judgment" (John 5. 27). He foretold that the
"hour is coming in the which all that are in
the graves shall hear His voice, and shall come
forth; they that have done good unto the
resurrection of life; and they that have done
evil unto the resurrection of damnation" (John
5. 28; 29). His hearers, scorning Him, put

Him to a felon's death, but in the Resurrection God vindicated all these claims. Hence Paul could say to that audience on Mars Hill that God "hath appointed a day, in the which He will judge the world in righteousness by that Man whom He hath ordained; whereof He hath given assurance unto all men, in that He hath raised Him from the dead" (Acts 17. 31).

JUSTIFIED IN CHRIST.

(4) *Moreover, the Resurrection is the token that those very persons, who, as sinners, are destined to stand at that judgment bar, can, through believing in Jesus, be justified from all things, and stand righteous before God.* In Romans 4. 25, we learn that He "was delivered for our offences, and was raised again for our justification"; or, as one old rendering has it, "was delivered because we had offended, and was raised again because we are justified." The One who said that He had come "to give His life a ransom for many" (Mark 10. 45) did so on the Cross. But did God accept the ransom-price? The answer is a risen and

G

exalted Christ! As has been aptly said : "I look at the Cross, and know atonement made; I look at the open sepulchre and know atonement accepted."

A man is convicted for some offence, and sentenced to a fine or imprisonment. He is held in custody until his fine is forthcoming, when he is immediately liberated. But no receipt is needed or given for that fine. The free man is the guarantee of the paid fine. So the Son of God, as our Surety, was delivered on account of our guilt to the grasp of unwavering Justice, and went down into the prison-house of death. That awful debt of sin He paid, in all its terrible entirety, and the divine receipt is a Discharged Prisoner, a resurrected Christ, in whom we rejoice, singing :

> He paid on the tree
>   The sentence for me,
> And now both the Surety
> And sinner are free.

XII.

MORE FRUITS OF THE RESURRECTION.

WE have considered some of the blessings which accrue to the believer in virtue of the Resurrection of the Son of God. A few more demand our attention.

(5) *The raising from the dead of our Lord Jesus is the pledge of the eternal security of all who by faith have become united to Him, and the dynamic of a new life in the power of the risen Christ.* The Saviour who died for us, is now for us at God's right hand, representing us there until the day when He will present us there. He is our great High Priest, who is "able also to save them to

the uttermost—'to all completeness'—that come unto God by Him, seeing He ever liveth to make intercession for them" (Heb. 7. 25). The Resurrection, therefore, is a call to a new life. Hence the Apostle exhorts : "If ye then be risen with Christ, seek those things which are above, where Christ sitteth on the right hand of God" (Col. 3. 1).

But it is more than an invitation; it is an incentive. It is the plea for a higher life, and the power that makes such attainable. So Paul writes : "Knowing that Christ, being raised from the dead, dieth no more; . . . likewise reckon ye also yourselves to be dead indeed unto sin, but alive unto God through Jesus Christ our Lord" (Rom. 6. 9-11).

> Jesus lives! For me He died;
> Then will I, to Jesus living,
> Pure in heart and act abide,
> Praise to Him and glory giving.

(6) *Again, the Resurrection is the only abiding source of comfort in the face of the last enemy, death.* That immortality which

has been the vision of poets, the dream of sages, and the desire of all, has been proclaimed a reality. The rising from the dead of the Lord Jesus is the effective guarantee of our resurrection and our reunion with friends who have fallen asleep, of whom it can be said: "These all died in faith" (Heb. 11. 13). Accordingly, while we may sorrow, it is not with that numbing despair of "others who have no hope;" for "if we believe that Jesus died and rose again, even so them also which sleep in Jesus will God bring with Him" (1 Thess. 4. 14). Hence, writing to believers at Corinth, Paul declares His assurance that "He which raised up the Lord Jesus shall raise up us also by Jesus, and shall present us with you" (2 Cor. 4. 14).

In the Vatican at Rome is a long gallery, on one side of which are sculptured epitaphs to the heathen dead, and, on the other side, similar mementos of departed Christians. Among the former is a magnificent group of lions leaping upon horses, the emblem of destruction. On the opposite wall is depicted the Good Shepherd, tenderly carrying a lamb in His bosom, with this inscription underneath : "Alexander is not dead, but lives beyond the stars." Between the thoughts embodied in these two sculptured groups stands the vacant tomb of the risen Redeemer.

But His Resurrection is more than the pledge of ours. It is also the pattern of it. Even the noblest of the old-time philosophers regarded man's body as a clog and burden to his soul. Thus Plotinus was thankful that "he was not tied to an immortal body." But that which philosophy would destroy, the power of the Gospel of Christ transfigures; and of this His Resurrection is both the earnest and the guarantee.

Therefore it is that Christians pray, not for the annihilation of the body, but for its ennobling; not for its destruction, but for its glorification. Like Paul, "We that are in this tabernacle do groan, being burdened; not for that we would be unclothed, but clothed upon, that mortality may be swallowed up of life" (2 Cor. 5. 4). Nor will this groaning be unanswered, nor this desire unrealized. For our hope is centred in the "Saviour, the Lord Jesus Christ, who shall fashion anew the body of our humiliation, that it may be conformed to the body of His glory; according to the working whereby He is able even to subject all things unto Himself" (Phil. 3. 21, R.V.).

INCORRUPTIBLE INHERITANCE.

(7) Finally, the Resurrection of our Lord Jesus Christ is not only the supreme comfort in the lone hour of bereavement, but is also the unfailing guarantee of the future blessedness of the believer in that realm where "there shall be no more death, neither sorrow, nor crying," when the "former things are passed away" (Rev. 21. 4). On the even of His departure from them by the rugged way of the Cross, the Lord comforted His disciples with these memorable words: "Let not your heart be troubled: ye believe in God, believe also in Me. In My Father's house are many mansions: if it were not so I would have

told you. I go to prepare a place for you.
And if I go and prepare a place for you,
I will come again, and receive you unto
Myself; that where I am, there ye may be
also" (John 14. 1-3). Of this sweetest of
promises, pressed out by love from the bleeding
heart of the Redeemer some hours before
Calvary, the initial step toward fulfilment was
His victorious Resurrection with His subsequent
glorious ascension into heaven, His "going to
prepare a place."

Writing to the Thessalonian Church, Paul
speaks of the dominating purpose in their
lives after they had "turned to God from idols
to serve the living and true God" (1 Thess.
1. 9). It was "to wait for His Son from
heaven, whom He raised from the dead, even
Jesus" (1. 10).   In that verse the Holy
Spirit conjoins the Resurrection of our Lord
Jesus with His coming again, couples "the
Hope of the Promise" with "the Blessed
Hope."

It was when contemplating the grace of

God in Jesus Christ, that Peter, thrilled with the immensity of it all, burst into a rapturous song of praise, saying: "Blessed be the God and Father of our Lord Jesus Christ, which according to His abundant mercy hath begotten us again unto a living hope, by the Resurrection of Jesus Christ from the dead, to an inheritance incorruptible, and undefiled, and that fadeth not away, reserved in heaven for you, who are kept by the power of God, through faith, unto salvation" (1 Peter 1. 3-5).

And the culmination of all this blessedness lies in these words: "You unto Myself." In them we have climbed the ascent of the mount of the Lord, and now stand upon the apex of the eternal purposes, far above the mists which shroud the valleys below, and merged in the cloudless sunshine of His everlasting love. For then "shall we ever be with the Lord" (1 Thess. 4. 17).

With Him in glory! O wonderful word!
Eye hath not seen, and ear hath not heard,
Mind hath not fathomed the future in store,
Reserved for the children of God evermore.

Suffering over, and failure, and sin,
Like Him without, and like Him within;
Bodies made perfect, and spirits set free,
We'll share in that glory, whose glory we see.

With Him in glory, beholding His face!
With Him in glory! O marvellous grace!
Holy, and happy, and reigning in bliss!
Can there be anything greater than this?

XIII.

THE SCRIPTURES AND THE RESURRECTION.

WE have already noticed that our Lord Jesus Christ foretold, on no fewer than seven occasions, that He would rise from the dead. But, writing to the Church at Corinth, Paul goes further, for he declares expressly that the Resurrection was "according to the Scriptures" (1 Cor. 15. 4). At that period, the "Scriptures" could denote only the books of the Old Testament. Therefore, the Apostle's claim is that the Resurrection had been fore-shown in those books. This claim, moreover, Christ Himself and established as true, when, after He had risen, He said: "These are the words which I spake unto you while I was yet with you, that all things must be fulfilled which were written in the law of Moses, and in the Prophets, and in the Psalms, concerning Me" (Luke 24. 44).

Hence it was that Paul was able at Antioch to preach "Christ crucified," and to add : "And we declare unto you glad tidings, how that the promise which was made unto the fathers, God hath fulfilled the same unto us their children, in that He hath raised up Jesus again" (Acts 13. 32, 33). Plainly, he was asserting that the Resurrection was the fulfilment of an Old Testament promise of God.

Prophesied in the Pentateuch.

This same assertion Paul made before King Agrippa, saying : "I stand and am judged for the hope of the promise made of God unto our fathers. . . . Why should it be thought a thing incredible with you, that God should raise the dead?" (Acts 26. 6-8). Then he added : "Having, therefore, obtained help of God, I continue unto this day, witnessing both to small and great, saying none other things than those which the prophets and Moses did say should come, That Christ should suffer, and that He should be the first that should rise from the dead" (Acts 26. 22-23). In other words, Jesus Christ taught, and through His servant affirmed, that His bodily resurrection had been foreshadowed in the Books of Moses, the Pentateuch; in the Prophets; and in the Psalms; that is—since these three constituted the Jewish divisions of the Book—throughout the Old Testament.

On both the occasions just mentioned, then, Paul taught that the death and resurrection of Christ were the fulfilling of a "promise." Early in the Book of Genesis, we read of a promise made by God in the presence of disobedient and dejected Adam, that the Seed of the woman would bruise the enemy, while Himself being bruised (3. 15). This was the first definite announcement that the incarnate Son of God would one day, "through death," destroy "him that had the power of death, that is, the devil" (Heb. 2. 14). It was the first grey dawn carried by the far-flung rays of the rising sun of redemption. It foretold Christ crucified.

But later in this same Book is found another promise. It was that with which God cheered pilgrim Abraham, saying that in him "shall all families of the earth be blessed" (12. 3). But this promise could only be made good through the line of Isaac, who was, in picture, received back as from the dead. Accordingly, after the offering of Isaac at Mount Moriah, the promise is renewed to Abraham in these words: "In thy seed shall all the nations of the earth be blessed" (Gen. 22. 18).

ISAAC, TYPE OF CHRIST.

The commentary of the Holy Spirit upon this promise is found in the Epistle to the Hebrews: "By faith Abraham, when he was tried, offered up Isaac: and he that had received the promises offered up his only-begotten son, of whom it was said, That in Isaac shall thy seed be called: Accounting that God was able to raise him up, even from the dead; from whence also he received him in a figure." Isaac, therefore, raised to life from the altar of sacrifice, that through him the blessing of

God might flow to the world, is an old-time picture of a risen Christ. And so this latter promise outlined the Resurrection.

Turn now in thought to Genesis 8. 4: "And the ark rested in the seventh month, on the 17th day of the month, upon the mountains of Ararat." That ark, the means of salvation in the judgment-storms of God's anger, is a figure of Jesus Christ our Saviour. Isaiah understood it to be so, for he wrote: "A man shall be as an hiding-place from the wind, and a covert from the tempest" (Isa. 32. 2). Peter, too, understood it to be so, for he couples together "the days of Noah while the ark was a-preparing," with "the Resurrection of Jesus Christ" (1 Pet. 3. 21), setting forth the ark as a type of the mystical death and resurrection of the believer, in Christ dead and risen.

In Exodus 12, the seventh month became by a divine order the first month of the year (v. 2), when Israel was redeemed from bondage by the blood of the Passover lamb, slain on the fourteenth day. In Lev. 23. 5,

6, the precise day is re-affirmed. On that first day of the feast, the Lord Jesus was betrayed (Matt. 26. 17), after observing the feast with His disciples, that is, on Thursday evening, the fourteenth Nisan. Early on Friday morning, the fifteenth Nisan, He was tried, condemned, and crucified. On Saturday, the sixteenth Nisan, His dead body lay in the cold tomb, and on Sunday, the seventeenth Nisan, He rose again in the power of an endless life.

Accordingly, as on a day noted by the inspired penman with meticulous care, the ark of Noah rested on the surface of a world new-swept by the floods; so, ages afterwards, on the anniversary of that very day, Christ the true Ark, having passed through the judgment, rested in the calm of Resurrection.

Again, in the thirteenth chapter of Leviticus are given the laws applicable to leprosy, while in the succeeding chapter is detailed the law of the cleansing of the leper. View the suggestive scene. A leper has been healed. The High Priest meets him outside the camp, taking two sparrows with him. One he slays in an earthen bowl over running water. The other he dips in the blood of its slain fellow, then liberates, and the Priest and the cleansed leper watch it as it wings its flight heaven- ward. This ceremony, enacted at the cleansing of a leper, was a simple picture of the means of cleansing the fouler leprosy of sin; for while the first bird depicts Him "who was delivered for our offences," the second declares that He was "raised again for our justification" (Rom. 4. 25).

A Sheaf of the First Fruits.

In the 23rd chapter of this same Book of Leviticus, God gives to the Israelites certain laws to be observed when they would come into their divinely-appointed inheritance in the land of Canaan. When the golden harvest days would roll round year by year, each Israelite was instructed to bring to the priest "a sheaf of the first fruits" of the harvest. Then the command continued: "He shall wave the sheaf before the Lord to be accepted for

H

you; on the morrow after the Sabbath the priest shall wave it" (v. 11).

The Holy Spirit, through the great apostle, gives the significance of this ritual, when he says: "But now is Christ risen from the dead, and become the first-fruits of them that slept" (1 Cor. 15. 20). For as these first-fruits were a sample of the whole harvest to follow, so the Resurrection of the Lord Jesus Christ is the pattern, to which, at His coming, every believer will be conformed. The irony of unbelief on the part of men becomes evident when it is remembered that, at the very time when the priests were waving this first-fruits' sheaf of wheat before the now-rent veil of the temple, as an offering to God, that One, who in His victorious Resurrection was in very truth the First-fruits, stood in the midst of His humble disciples in an upper room, having been rejected and done to death by the organized religion of His day.

Further down in the same chapter, at verse 15, these words occur: "Ye shall count unto you from the morrow after the Sabbath."

As the Sabbath commemorated the first and material creation, so the "morrow after the Sabbath," or the first day of the week, marks the Resurrection, and the resultant new and spiritual creation, for the Apostle writes: "If any man be in Christ, he is a new creation" (2 Cor. 5. 17).

The Resurrection, therefore, was, in figure, "written in the law of Moses" (Luke 24. 44).

The 53rd Chapter of Isaiah.
The Book of Hosea.
The Sign of Jonah.
The Testimony of David and the Psalms.

XIV.

MORE ABOUT THE SCRIPTURES
AND THE RESURRECTION.

HAVING considered the Resurrection of
our Lord as found in promise and in
picture in the writings of Moses, we shall
pursue our quest for it in the prophetical
books.

In that entrancing fifty-third chapter of
Isaiah are graphically described the sufferings
and death of the Lord Jesus, the One on
whom the Lord "made to strike" the "iniquity
of us all" (v. 6). In verse 9, we are brought
to the garden tomb, and we learn that He
was "with the rich in His death." Then we
are told : "Yet it pleased the Lord to bruise
Him : He hath put Him to grief; when Thou
shalt make His soul an offering for sin"
(v. 10). Then follows the wonderful sequel :

"He shall see His seed, He shall prolong His days, and the pleasure of the Lord shall prosper in His hand. He shall see of the travail of His soul, and shall be satisfied" (v. 10, 11). This brings us beyond the tomb, to the triumph of His Resurrection.

Again, in the Book of Hosea, chapter 6, verse 2, these words are found: "After two days will He revive us; in the third day He will raise us up, and we shall live in His sight." In this declaration, which suggests both the fact and the time of the Resurrection, the Holy Spirit is regarding "all God's redeemed people as quickened together with Christ, and raised up together with Him."

THE SIGN OF JONAH.

Further, in the prophecy of Jonah, chapter 1, verse 15, we learn how the disobedient prophet, having brought the ship, in which he had hidden himself, near to destruction, was cast into the sea. Verse 17 tells us that "the Lord had prepared a great fish to swallow up Jonah. And Jonah was in the belly of the fish three days and three nights." Both the fact and the figure of Jonah were for ever fixed by Jesus Christ Himself. To certain of the Scribes and Pharisees seeking a sign from Him, He replied: "An evil and adulterous generation seeketh after a sign; and there shall no sign be given to it, but the sign of the prophet Jonas: For as Jonas was three days and three nights in the whale's belly; so shall the Son of Man be three days and three nights in the heart of the earth" (Matt. 12. 39, 40). In the second chapter of the book, thoughts are expressed which transcend all that was true of Jonah, and which find realization only in the death and resurrection of Christ. Verse 4 says: "I am cast out of Thy sight,"—pointing to the death of Christ—"yet I will look again toward Thy holy temple"—foretelling His Resurrection from the dead.

Again, in verse 6 are the words: "I went down to the bottoms of the mountains; the earth with her bars was about Me for ever," once more setting forth the Lord Jesus Christ descending into death; while the verse closes with the words : "Yet hast Thou brought up my life from corruption," indicating the fact of His Resurrection. Accordingly, the Resurrection was written, too, "in the prophets" (Luke 24. 44).

Now turn to the Psalms. In Psalm 2, the "kings of the earth set themselves, and the rulers take counsel together, against the Lord, and against His Anointed" (v. 2). In the Gospels, we learn that this resulted in Christ being crucified. In verse 7, God vindicates His Anointed, saying : "Thou art My Son; this day have I begotten Thee." Nor are we left to conjecture who is "the Anointed," and in what way He has been "begotten" by God, for Paul, preaching at Antioch, says : "God hath fulfilled the same unto us, their children, in that He hath raised up Jesus again; as it is also written in the second Psalm, 'Thou art My Son; this day have I begotten Thee'" (Acts 13. 33). The "Son" is, therefore, Jesus Christ, and the "day," that third and resurrection day.

THE TESTIMONY OF DAVID.

Again, read Psalm 16, from verse 8: "I have set the Lord always before me: because He is at my right hand, I shall not be moved, Therefore my heart is glad, and my glory rejoiceth; my flesh also shall rest in hope: For Thou wilt not leave my soul in hell; neither wilt Thou suffer Thine Holy One to see corruption."

Here, too, we are left in no doubt as to the Person referred to in these verses, for Peter, speaking of "Jesus of Nazareth," who was "crucified and slain," but "whom God hath raised up, having loosed the pains of death," says that "David speaketh concerning Him," and proceeds to quote the above verses from the sixteenth Psalm (Acts 2. 22-25). In them is presented a compendium of the earthly life and work of the Son of God, "who for the joy that was set before Him, endured the Cross, despising the shame, and is set down at the right hand of the throne of God" (Heb. 12. 2).

In verse 10, the word "hell" is "sheol," equivalent to the Greek word "hades," and signifies the place of the dead. In the same verse, the soul and body of the Lord Jesus are distinguished. As to His soul, the prophetic writer says: "Thou wilt not leave My soul in hades." As to His body he adds: "Neither wilt Thou suffer Thine Holy One to see corruption." In verse 10, we have the death of Christ, followed by "sheol" and the grave, the "cross" and the "shame" spoken of in Hebrews 12. Then in verse 11, we have the "joy that was set before Him," life, fullness of joy, the right hand of God, and pleasures for evermore.

Take now Psalm 22, which is essentially the Psalm of the Cross, beginning, as it does, with the cry of the stricken Lamb, "My God, My God, why hast Thou forsaken Me?" and ending with the words "that he hath done," or, as it might be rendered, "that it is finished." From verses 1 to 20 are pictured the sorrows and death-agonies of Christ. Then verse 21 reads: "Thou hast heard Me," proving an accepted Sacrifice. Hence in verse 22 come the words: "I will declare Thy name unto my brethren; in the midst of the congregation will I praise Thee," speaking of the consequent glory of Resurrection, which was the effective answer of the One who "heard," to the plea of His well-beloved.

Finally, then, the Resurrection of the Lord Jesus Christ was written also "in the Psalms" (Luke 24. 44).

Therefore it is that the believer rejoices, not only in the knowledge that Christ "died for our sins according to the Scriptures; and that He was buried," but also in the assurance "that He rose again the third day according to the Scriptures" (1 Cor. 15. 3, 4). Well and truly has it been put thus: "As the Paschal sun arose from the chills and fogs of the sombre night, filling the earth with lustrous beauty, so, on that morning, Jesus ascended from the realms of death, and dispersed the awful gloom that enshrouded the moral world. Thus He resumed His power, recovered His challenged rights, regained His waning influence, reasserted His sacred grandeur; and answering thus His malignant enemies, sent echoing down the ages the blest assurance that there is something in the universe higher than its laws—namely, a Christ who could not be holden of them, but triumphed over them."

> There rose from death's dark gloom,
>   Unseen by mortal eye,
> Triumphant o'er the tomb,
>   The Lord of earth and sky.

XV.

OPPOSITION TO THE RESURRECTION.

IN all times there have been, outside the pale of the professed Church, unbelievers and opponents of God and the Bible. But that is not the characteristic of these present days. It is that, within the fold of the very Church itself, leaders are coming to the front, increasing in numbers as in boldness, to deny the things they once professed to hold dear. Yet this is the literal fulfilment of Scripture itself, for Paul, writing to Timothy, said: "Now the Spirit speaketh expressly that in the latter times some shall depart from the faith, giving heed to seducing spirits, and doctrines of demons; speaking lies in hypocrisy" (1 Tim. 4. 1, 2). When the amazing growth of spiritism

—"doctrines of demons"—is remembered, the wonderful prophetic accuracy of those verses of Scripture will be apparent.

Further, the same writer foretells that "the time will come when they will not endure sound doctrine; but after their own lusts shall they heap to themselves teachers, having itching ears; and they shall turn away their ears from the truth, and shall be turned unto fables" (2 Tim. 4. 3, 4). This is precisely what is happening to-day, when the pulpit commonly serves up teaching which accords with the wishes of the pew.

It seems as though the desire which laid hold of the human stock at its very head, a desire born of the suggestion of the tempter, "Ye shall be as God" (Gen. 3. 5, R.V.) has now reached full fruition, for religious leaders have dethroned God and enthroned man. They are most careful to tell us that Jesus Christ was a good man, but was nothing more than man. Yet they are equally careful to impress us with the idea that there is an "essential oneness of God and man," that indeed there is "no real

distinction between humanity and the Deity."
Thus they would humanize the Deity, and deify
humanity.

The greatest danger, then, to the Christian
Church of this age is not from the uncouth,
ribald infidel, but from the scholarly, religious
critic; not from without, but from within.

Yet these grand and glorious truths of the
Word of God, belaboured from without and
betrayed from within, still stand mighty and
majestic in the face of every opposing force.
"The wave with its froth passes away; the
rock stands firm." And towering high among
them, unshaken in its veracity and unlessened
in its vitality, is the fact of the literal resurrection of the Christ who was crucified. Only
in proportion as this truth is maintained and
proclaimed, will the individual Christian and
the collective Church experience the power of
God and fulfil the purpose of God. As one
has written : "To preach the fact of the Resurrection was the first function of the Evangelists;
to embody the doctrine of the Resurrection
is the great office of the Church; to learn the

meaning of the Resurrection is the task not of one age only, but of all."

In conclusion, this apostasy is an unmistakable sign of the near return of our Lord and Saviour, Jesus Christ. In view of this, surely the aim of every believer should be that he "may know Him, and the power of His Resurrection, and the fellowship of His sufferings, being made comformable to His death" (Phil. 3. 10). And should the reader of these pages be one who has not hitherto accepted Jesus Christ, by faith, as a personal Saviour, we would point such to these life-giving words . "If thou shalt confess with thy mouth the Lord Jesus, and shalt believe in thine heart that God hath raised Him from the dead, thou shalt be saved" (Rom. 10. 9).